Naomi Thornton
and André Amstutz

GRAFTON BOOKS

A Division of the Collins Publishing Group

LONDON GLASGOW
TORONTO SYDNEY AUCKLAND

Help Your Child To Write

All children love scribbling; turning scribbling into writing is easier than you think. These books will help you to help your child to write. Each one teaches a specific group of letters but you don't need to buy them all. The whole alphabet and practice patterns are printed at the end of all of them.

At first it is best to enjoy the stories and the pictures for themselves. Then, when the child knows the stories, you can use the characters and events to help him learn to write.

Here are some tips:
1. Have ready lots of paper (the books are not for writing in) and any kind of pencil, pen, felt-tip or crayon.
2. Only practise writing skills when your child is relaxed and in the mood. Respond to his need to learn, not your urge to teach.
3. Holding the pencil correctly like the child in the picture is a first step. Reverse the picture for a left-handed child.
4. All the books start with patterns. These are merely 'rhythmic scribbles' to be repeated until the child can draw them with ease. Each one gives practice in the movements needed for certain letters.

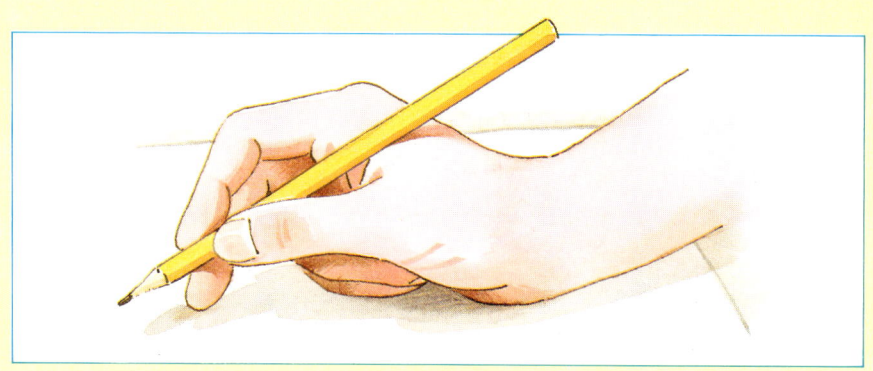

5. It is better for the child to repeat the patterns freely in his own style than to reproduce them accurately but unnaturally.
6. Don't worry about speed. The child will learn best at his own pace.
7. Watching you enjoy the patterns and letters he makes will be more fun for the child than working alone.
8. Remember, there's no need for paper. You can draw letters in the air, in the dust on the sideboard, in sand or on steamed-up windows.
9. When your child knows some letters, help him to use them. When he names an object, get him to write its name down. Get him to label his dog, his bed, his brother, his cup, his jumper. You name it, he can write it. And he'll have fun doing so.

Who is this on the roof?

Draw the rooftops like this:

Draw the house walls like this:

Draw the whole house like this:

It's Dizzy Wizzy the witch

Draw Dizzy's hat like this:

Draw her wand like this:

Dizzy Wizzy is a witch
But Dizzy cannot fly
She doesn't know the spell to use
To take off in the sky

Draw Dizzy like this:

Max is Dizzy Wizzy's cat
But Max is scared of heights
Even sitting on the roof
Gives him a nasty fright

Draw Max like this:

If only Dizzy knew the spell
To put them into flight
She and Max would have such fun
Among the stars at night

Draw the stars like this:

What we need is exercise
Said Dizzy to her cat
Sitting on this roof all night
Will make us very fat

I wish, I wish, I wish, I wish
I wish I knew the spell
Together, Max, we'd see the stars
We'd fly so very well

Write **x** for exercise like this:

Write **w** for wish like this:

'What's that awful noise?' asked Dizzy
Jumping from her seat
With her broomstick in one hand
And Max upon her feet

Wizzy, wuzzy, wuzzy, wizzy
Whizzed the dreadful sound
Buzzing near and buzzing far
Whizzing round and round

Write **z** for zzzzzz like this:

z z z z z z

Wizzy Wuzzy was a wasp
With a frightful sting
He stung the cat, he stung the witch
And made poor Dizzy sing
'Yaroo, varoom, yaroo, varoom'

Write **y** for yaroo like this:

y y y y y y

Yaroo, varoom, yaroo, varoom
She yelled with all her might
And suddenly the broom took off —
At last she was in flight

Max the cat forgot his fear
And jumped aboard the broom
Yaroo, varoom, yaroo, varoom
We're going to the moon

Write **y** and **v** like this:

y v y v y v y

And that's how Dizzy got to know
The spell to make a broomstick go

Can you write the magic spell
That Dizzy Wizzy learned to yell?

Write yaroo, varoom like this:

yaroo varoom

Now look at the other letters
of the alphabet, on the next page

Practise the patterns, letters and numbers

Grafton Books
A Division of the Collins Publishing Group
8 Grafton Street, London W1X 3LA

Published by Grafton Books 1986
Copyright © André Amstutz 1986

British Library Cataloguing in Publication Data
Thornton, Naomi
 Dizzy Witch. – (Help Your Child To Write; 2)
 1. English language – Alphabet – Juvenile literature.
 I. Title II. Amstutz, André III. Series
 421'.1   PE1155
 ISBN 0-246-12938-7 (Hardback)
 ISBN 0-583-30996-8 (Paperback)

Printed in Spain by Graficas Reunidas

All rights reserved. No part of this publication
may be reproduced, stored in a retrieval system, or
transmitted, in any form or by any means, electronic,
mechanical, photocopying, recording or otherwise,
without prior permission of the publishers.